This is Our History

To my Dad, who continually tells us stories about his childhood in West Africa Ghana.

Thank you for getting on the ship in April 1975 in Ivory Coast,

the step you took paved the way for many generations.

Africans & African Americans,

What is Black history?

Black history is this: you are from

a rich line of kings and queens

tracing back to the great continent of

Africa.

That makes you

a Prince or a **Princess.**

The journey from our homeland was long, but our ancestors worked very hard to make sure we would have a

Bright Future

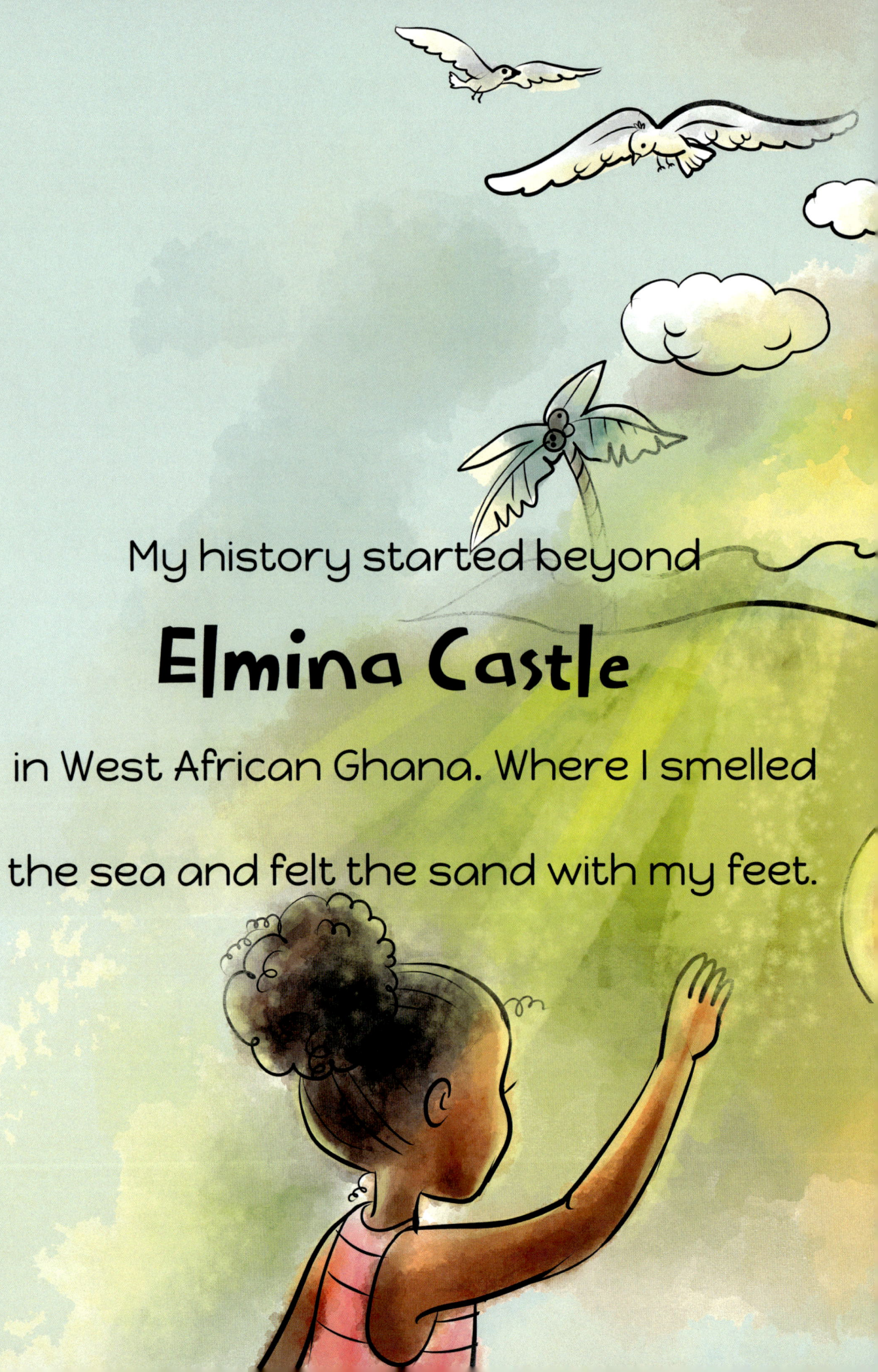

My history started beyond

Elmina Castle

in West African Ghana. Where I smelled the sea and felt the sand with my feet.

I am from rich soil,

a land filled with so many

Treasures.

There are many nations.

I stand out in so many ways because I am **royalty.**

Royalty runs through my veins.

As a Prince or a Princess, I will grow to become a **King**

When I look in the mirror, I see all that I can be! I have a

Bright Future

ahead of me.

ARCH

ASTRONAUT

TEACHER

I am going to make my ancestors,

my family and the world

Proud.

Africans, African Americans, what is Black History? Black history is you!

"Remember who you are." As the great lion said to his cub.

I know my history.

Therefore

I know who I am.

HISTORICAL FACTS

ELMINA CASTLE

ELMINA CASTLE IS A HISTORICAL SITE, LOCATED ON THE SHORES OF WEST AFRICA, GHANA.

THIS CASTLE WAS USED TO HOLD MANY AFRICANS,

AGAINST THEIR WILL, BEFORE THEY WERE TAKEN AWAY TO UNKNOWN LANDS.

"DOOR OF NO RETURN"

THE SIGN THAT READS "DOOR OF NO RETURN" IS STILL LOCATED ON A DOOR OUTSIDE OF

ELMINA CASTLE, FACING THE OCEAN VIEW. THIS IS THE LAST DOOR OUR ANCESTORS

WENT THROUGH BEFORE BEING FORCED INTO THE SHIPS.

COCOA BEANS

COCOA BEANS ARE ONE OF THE MAIN AGRICULTURAL RESOURCES IN GHANA.

GHANA IS AMONG THE LARGEST EXPORTERS OF COCOA BEANS IN THE WORLD.

PRAYER TO HELP IN TIME OF NEED

Our Father in heaven, hallowed be Your name.

Your kingdom come,

Your will be done on earth as it is in heaven.

Give us this day our daily bread,

and forgive us our debts,

as we also have forgiven our debtors.

Lead us not into temptation, but deliver us from evil.

For Thine is the kingdom, the power and the glory.

Forever and ever amen.

THIS IS OUR

I am **CREATED IN THE IMAGE OF GOD**

I know my History, therefore I know who I am.

I am **BORN IN GREATNESS.**

I know my History, therefore I know who I am.

I am the **OFFSPRING OF KINGS AND QUEENS.**

I know my History, therefore I know who I am.

I am a **LEADER.**

I know my History, therefore I know who I am.

HISTORY

I am a **CHANGE MAKER**.

I know my History, therefore I know who I am.

I am a **MASTERPIECE**, the **CENTERPIEC**e.

I know my History, therefore I know who I am.

I am **CONFIDENT**.

I know my History, therefore I know who I am.

I am **PHENOMENAL**.

I know my History, therefore I know who I am.

This Is Our History:

Humansville Series

Published by Vncbooks, LLC

www.vncbooks.com

West Orange, New Jersey

Text Copyright 2022 Virtuous Nyamesem Cornwall

Illustration Copyright 2022 Emanuela Ntamack

All rights reserved. No part of this publication may be reproduced, distributed, or transmitted in any form or by any means, including photocopying, recording, or other electronic or mechanical methods, without the prior written permission of the Publisher, except in the case of brief quotation embodied in critical reviews and certain other noncommercials uses permitted by copyright law. For permission requests, write to the publisher, www.vncbooks.com

Library of Congress Control Number 2022901267

Paperback ISBN: 978-1-7341747-6-2

Discounts are available for quantity purchases, and for schools or associations. All inquires can be sent to the author.

For information or to book an Author visit, please go to www.vncbooks.com

Made in the USA
Middletown, DE
31 January 2023

23662618R00018